STUDENT UNIT GUIDE

Edexcel A2 | UNIT 3

Economics

Business Economics and
Economic Efficiency

Marwan Mikdadi

Philip Allan Updates, an imprint of Hodder Education, an Hachette UK company, Market Place, Deddington, Oxfordshire, OX15 0SE

Orders

Bookpoint Ltd, 130 Milton Park, Abingdon, Oxfordshire, OX14 4SB
tel: 01235 827827
fax: 01235 400401
e-mail: education@bookpoint.co.uk
Lines are open 9.00 a.m.–5.00 p.m., Monday to Saturday, with a 24-hour message answering service. You can also order through the Philip Allan Updates website: www.philipallan.co.uk

First printed 2009
Impression number 5
Year 2013 2012 2011

This Guide has been written specifically to support students preparing for the Edexcel A2 Economics Unit 3 examination. The content has been neither approved nor endorsed by Edexcel and remains the sole responsibility of the author.

Typeset by Phoenix Photosetting, Chatham, Kent
Printed by MPG Books, Bodmin

Hachette UK's policy is to use papers that are natural, renewable and recyclable products and made from wood grown in sustainable forests. The logging and manufacturing processes are expected to conform to the environmental regulations of the country of origin.

P1535

Contents

Introduction

Aims 4

How to use this guide and the exam format 4

Assessment objectives 5

Revision 6

How to answer supported multiple-choice questions 9

How to answer data-response questions 10

How to evaluate 12

■ ■ ■

Content Guidance

About this section 14

Firms 15

Costs and revenues 18

Motives of the firm 24

Theory of the firm 28

Competition policy 40

■ ■ ■

Questions and Answers

About this section 44

Supported multiple-choice questions

Costs and revenues 45

Motives of the firm 46

Theory of the firm: perfect competition 46

Theory of the firm: monopolistic competition 47

Theory of the firm: oligopoly 47

Theory of the firm: monopoly 48

Competition policy 49

Supported multiple-choice answers 49

Data-response questions

Q1 Royal Mail must 'face the facts' of sell-off 53

Q2 Tesco wins appeal against Competition Commission test for new sites 57

Q3 Trains cost 50% more than in rest of Europe 61

Introduction

Aims

This guide has been written specifically to prepare students studying for Unit 3 of Edexcel's A2 GCSE examination in economics: Business Economics and Economic Efficiency. It provides an overview of the knowledge and particular skills required to achieve a good grade in the examination.

The unit's aim is to consider the role firms play in the economy, their size, how they behave and what actions the government may take to regulate them.

The theoretical content has been divided up into five main topics.
(1) Firms
(2) Costs and revenues
(3) Motives of the firm
(4) Theory of the firm
(5) Competition policy

How to use this guide and the exam format

The guide is designed to give a summary of the key areas that are likely to be assessed in Unit 3, with a focus on how these can then be applied to the examination. There are a number of sample questions included in the last section with actual answers written by students. These are marked with explanatory comments, which highlight weaknesses and areas that students can revise before the examination. This guide should be used only in conjunction with your textbooks, class notes and other materials that you have discussed and used in class with your teacher.

Unit 3 will account for 40% of the total mark obtainable at A2. It is worth 80 uniform mark system (UMS) marks, as compared to Unit 4, which is worth 120 UMS marks. UMS marks are used to ensure that different exams can be compared more easily. Therefore, to obtain 80 UMS marks, a candidate does not need to score 72 (or 100%) in their exam. Full UMS marks are calculated by doubling the difference between the A and B grade boundaries and adding this to the A grade.

The exam will have two sections: the first comprises supported multiple-choice questions and the second data-response questions. The first section will contain eight supported multiple-choice questions. In the second section you will have to answer one data-response question from a choice of two. The exam lasts 1 hour and 30 minutes.

The supported multiple-choice section has 32 marks available, out of a possible 72. On that basis, it equals 45% of the available marks. You should, therefore, aim to spend no longer than 40 minutes on this section; that is about 5 minutes per question. It is very important that students stick to their timings: it is much easier to pick up a few marks on subsequent questions than trying to gain an additional mark on an earlier one. It is the law of diminishing marginal returns at work.

The data-response section will be marked out of 40 and will be worth 55% of your overall mark in the module. You should, therefore, aim to spend about 50 minutes on this, including reading through the extracts to make the right decision regarding which question you answer. Make sure you use the reading time wisely. Students cannot afford to start one question, only to decide halfway through that they wish they had attempted the other question. Therefore, make sure you read the questions, as well as making a note of how the data can be used to answer them.

As a rough guide based on the current examinations, a candidate can expect to get an A grade with an answer scoring more than 70%; in other words, 51 out of 72. However, this figure is finally determined after all the scripts have been marked, based on the examiners' view of the difficulty of the paper and the quality of the candidates sitting the paper.

June 2010 will see the introduction of the A* grade for the first time. This means that candidates will be expected to have scored an average of 90% across their two A2 modules (that is 180 of the available 200 UMS marks) and at least 320 UMS marks overall (in other words, at least an A grade for the A-level). This means that a candidate does not need to have an A grade at AS to obtain an A* at A2, although in practice it is unlikely that a candidate will score 90% at A2 and not have an A grade at AS.

It is worth remembering that both units at A2 contain **synoptic** elements; in other words they draw on links from the AS modules. When you have the chance, mention consumer surplus or price elasticities of demand to ensure that you refer to some of the concepts from Unit 1. Clearly, not all the synoptic elements need signposting. For example, you will be using your knowledge of demand and supply when considering the costs of a firm.

The final section of the book contains a number of supported multiple-choice and data-response questions. Use these to support your revision. These supported multiple-choice questions have been divided into topics corresponding to the four topics identified earlier: firms; costs and revenues; motives and theory of the firm; and competition policy. After revision of a topic attempt these questions, ideally under timed conditions, to ensure you have understood the topic.

Assessment objectives

There are four assessment objectives which examiners use when constructing the examination. A lot of care is taken in preparing an examination to make sure that all these objectives are assessed. It is, therefore, essential that you review the appropriate command words to ensure that you are following the instructions. Too often the biggest single weakness in a script is that the candidate fails to answer the question set, focusing instead on the one they wished to see or had prepared in class. That is never going to be the most successful strategy.

The assessment objectives are **knowledge**, **application**, **analysis** and **evaluation**. Throughout A2, evaluation has a more important role than at AS. In this unit it is equal to 18 out of the 40 marks available in the data-response section (i.e. 45%). There are no marks for evaluation available in the supported multiple-choice section.

	AO1 Knowledge 25%	AO2 Application 25%	AO3 Analysis 25%	AO4 Evaluation 25%
Supported multiple-choice questions	11	11	10	0
Data-response questions	7	7	8	18
Total	18	18	18	18

The examiners must allocate marks across the supported multiple-choice and data-response questions so that they fit the table above.

Command words

These are designed to give you an indication of the assessment objective being tested.

'Define', 'outline' and 'distinguish': these words focus on knowledge (AO1). Candidates are expected to define terms such as 'economies of scale', 'concentration ratios', 'barriers to entry' and 'allocative efficiency'.

'Analyse' and 'explain': these words direct the student toward the application (AO2) and analysis (AO3). One of the easiest ways to obtain the marks available when answering this sort of question is to use a diagram. The opportunity to apply the data and any real-world examples you may have discussed in class should be used to either support or illustrate your argument.

'Comment', 'contrast' and 'examine': the emphasis here is on a combination of analysis (AO3) and evaluation (AO4). If the word 'likely' is used, this suggests greater emphasis on evaluation, as in 'Comment on the likely effects...' The phrase implies there is an element of doubt as to whether the effects will actually occur and this doubt should be reflected in your answer.

'Assess', 'discuss', 'to what extent' and 'evaluate': the emphasis here is clearly on the need to evaluate (AO4). These questions will often have a high evaluative content. There needs to be some attempt to weigh up both sides of the argument and to form some judgment.

Revision

Revision is important to ensure success. Starting your revision as early as possible will improve your chance of success in the examination. Practice of past questions is essential; your teacher should be able supply you with past questions from the old Unit 4 exam paper. There will be little difference between these types of questions and those you will meet in the exam.

A revision schedule is included to offer some guidance. However, revision is a personal thing — a revision schedule should be designed to suit each student and should include rewards and milestones. Also be realistic — no one is going to revise effectively for 6 hours in a row. Don't fool yourself. You are better revising in short bursts, followed by regular self-testing.

It is important to revise topics early and often. All the evidence points to students having a better understanding of their notes and remembering them more effectively if they undertake the learning of a topic more than once. It is important, therefore, that you review all your notes during the Christmas break for a winter examination and the Easter break for a summer examination. This may seem like quite a long lead up to the exams but it also allows you to spot anything you are unsure of and remedy it in plenty of time.

At the start of your revision you should:

(1) Get a copy of the specification. This can be used as a checklist of the topics that you should study. The new specification clearly states what the student should be able to do before they can successfully undertake the examination. Make sure you recognise all the topics and that these have been covered in school. The specification can be downloaded from the Edexcel website at **www.edexcel.com**

(2) Check your notes. Using the specification, check you have the notes for each topic. Get the notes filed properly.

(3) Revise notes. Active revision is essential to ensure success. Simply reading your notes while listening to your iPod is unlikely to be good preparation. You may feel you have been working hard and this may have been sufficient to get you through your GCSEs, but it is not the reliable approach for A-level. Different people have different approaches to learning things by heart: condensing notes, writing lists of points, using mind-maps. Whichever way you think suits you, it is essential that, by the end of April (for summer exams) and the end of December (for winter exams), you are in a position to produce a list of topics and key points for each topic. Once this has been learnt, it will be much easier to return to your 'new' revision notes and revise these again.

(4) Practise past questions. Your teacher should provide you with past papers — use these wisely. It is important that you take the opportunity to answer them under timed conditions. Using mark schemes or your teacher's comments, learn from your mistakes. Identify the areas that you cannot do and then either revise them again or ask your teacher for assistance.

(5) Don't choose to revise only a few topics. You have to revise each topic in the specification. There are eight compulsory questions and these examine a range of topics from the whole specification. You cannot afford to try to question-spot and revise certain topics, otherwise you can be sure that you will be throwing away marks.

(6) Refresh your script. Try to make your answer stand out from the crowd. You could do this by having some real examples up your sleeve and using these to illustrate the point you are making, especially in the data-response section. You can get lots of examples from newspapers, television news programmes or the business pages of the BBC news website and blogs that BBC journalists write.

Revision planning

Plan your revision. There is no substitute for a well-ordered plan. In the final weeks leading up to the examination, you should start to revise the material you learnt over the Christmas or Easter holidays. Remember to spend a certain amount of time per module. If you were to spend about 45 minutes per module each day (assuming you are revising for six A2 modules), then this would be about 4½ hours a day in addition to school. Once you are on study leave then this can be increased, but remember to take regular breaks, otherwise you are likely to lose concentration and the time spent will be unproductive.

Suggested revision plan

Week 1	(a) Firms: why and how they grow and why some remain small. Barriers to entry
	(b) Costs and revenues, economies of scale and efficiency
	(c) Objectives of the firm: profit maximisation, sales maximisation and revenue maximisation
Week 2	(a) Concentration ratios
	(b) Perfect competition
	(c) Monopoly and price discrimination
Week 3	(a) Monopolistic competition
	(b) Oligopoly, collusion and use of non-price competition
	(c) Contestable markets
Week 4	(a) Pricing strategies: predatory pricing, limit pricing and cost plus pricing
	(b) Competition policy
	(c) Regulation of privatised industries

Always follow up a topic by doing some questions to see how much you can remember. Use the supported multiple-choice questions in the Question and Answer section of this book to help you.

Ask your teacher for some past papers to provide practice — remember the first examination in this module takes place in January 2010. Exams set between January 2002 and June 2009 in industrial economics with supported multiple-choice questions are still an excellent way to revise.

How to answer supported multiple-choice questions

There are eight compulsory supported multiple-choice questions, each worth 4 marks. One mark is for selecting the correct answer and the remaining 3 marks are available for your explanation.

Definitions are an easy way to obtain a mark. Often questions will have 1 mark for the definition of the key element of economics being examined. It is, therefore, essential that you learn your definitions. The glossary at the end of this book provides a useful start.

You can obtain a maximum of 3 marks if you select the wrong letter. Never leave an answer blank, however confused you are, as a definition can get 1 mark and these marks will all contribute to your overall performance.

You can also get up to 2 marks for explaining why two of the options are incorrect, but you must refer explicitly to the letter of the answer you are rejecting and also explain why you are rejecting it.

Annotate any diagrams that the examiners have given you. Where they haven't provided a diagram, consider whether you can draw one to support your answer. There is often a mark for shading in a key part of a diagram or highlighting something on a diagram that you draw. It is often easier to explain your answer with an accurately labelled diagram than with a long piece of continuous prose.

Remember the time allocation you have. Stick to it carefully. No more than 40 minutes should be spent on the supported multiple-choice section. If you spend too long here, it may mean you are not able to finish the data-response questions. Avoid spending too long on one question. This can cause you to lose the opportunity to score on another question. Even if you are unsure, select a letter and define the key terms. You can always come back to the question if you have spare time at the end. *Never leave an answer blank — select a letter — you can only gain by doing this.*

The best way to prepare for the supported multiple-choice section is to practise questions. There are limitations to the imagination of the examiners. If you see enough supported multiple-choice questions, you will begin to see what the examiner is looking for and possibly even become familiar with the style of the questions that might crop up in your exam.

The best approach to supported multiple-choice is to try to determine the answer before reading the options. By doing this, you are able to check that you are selecting the correct option.

Always check you have read the question properly — perhaps consider reading it a few times to ensure that you have understood exactly what is required from you. Make sure you understand the instructions to avoid falling into any traps that have been set. Show any workings; examiners may be able to find you a mark for part of your workings, even if you have eventually got the wrong answer. The job of an examiner is to mark everything on the page and give you the best possible mark you deserve.

How to answer data-response questions

There are two data-response questions in the examination, from which you have to answer one. Remember that you have 50 minutes in which to answer the question.

How to choose your question

The data-response question is likely to be made up of four parts with a heavy emphasis on evaluation in the last three parts. Remember to read the questions before you read the data. You should spend about 5 minutes choosing the question you wish to answer. This is so that:

- you can determine whether or not you can answer all the questions
- you are able to read the data knowing how it can be used to answer the questions

All Edexcel data-response questions are based on real-life examples. In recent years the questions have considered the banking, airline, confectionery, water, car and ice-cream industries. It is, therefore, worth reading a quality newspaper or business website to develop a good idea of the major industrial changes. Often the background understanding, although not essential, will give you a head-start over other candidates.

How to use the data and extract

When examiners write the question papers, they spend hours ensuring that every paragraph, piece of data and graph they include is helpful in answering the question set. It is vital, therefore, that you use the data and extract to help you answer the questions. It may be that the information is included as background or it may give you a steer as to the sort of answers the examiners are expecting. If the instructions in the question paper direct you to use the information — for instance, by saying 'with reference to extract one...', it is worth your while doing so, as there are certainly some marks reserved for this. However, avoid quoting too much from the data or extract, unless it is directly relevant to the answer that you are giving, as this will just waste valuable time. It is also worth using a number of highlighters to distinguish for your benefit between pieces of the information provided, so you can refer to it quickly during the exam. This is especially useful when answering questions under time pressure.

Analysing data

Data should be handled in a particular way. It is important that you try to manipulate it to help you answer the question. For example, you may be asked questions such as 'Consider the trend that the data exhibits', 'Calculate the percentage change' or 'Calculate the market share of a firm' from the data given to you. In these cases, avoid analysing the data by considering what has happened year-by-year. It is better to look at the overall picture compared to a detailed review and then draw conclusions.

Make sure you understand the data and charts fully. What are the axes telling you? Is this a percentage increase or is the subject matter measured in thousands or millions? Always check whether the data shows a firm's sales falling or rising less quickly. Be willing to use the data, calculate percentage changes and work out the trend over the time frame described.

Be willing to challenge the data. What is the source? Could it be biased? Is it too short a period of time to give a definitive understanding of the position the business or industry faces? What more information would you like to see to give you a better understanding of the firm or industry?

Hints on answering questions

Answers should be set within a theoretical context. Consider which part of the specification the examiner is trying to test, but remember to answer in the context of the data or the extract. A question on contestability in the airline industry (see Edexcel specimen paper available at **www.edexcel.com**) is never going to score highly if the answer given is purely theoretical. Think about the context and use your wider knowledge to support your answer. Consider the different airlines — for example, British Airways, Ryanair and easyJet — that you will have read about and use your own understanding of the airline industry.

It is crucial to define key terms; these can be the easiest marks to get and they are often ignored.

Responses must be presented from an economic angle. Too often, generalised descriptive, non-specialist observations are put forward by candidates which do not make use of what you have been taught.

Use diagrams to explain your answers. Sometimes examiners will demand these, but be willing to offer them regardless of whether you have been asked for them. Make sure they are clearly drawn and clearly labelled. The Edexcel marking system 'ePen' scans your work in black and white, so it is not possible to see colours or highlighter pen clearly. If you make a mistake, draw the diagram again: never use a diagram with some lines crossed out as it is hard to understand and is not clear to the examiners, so could cost you marks.

Evaluation

The last three parts of each question will contain evaluation. There are 40 marks available in the data response and 18 of these will test the higher-order skill of evaluation. No question will have more than 50% evaluation, which means that almost certainly each question will have at least half of it dedicated to evaluation.

It is possible that each part of a data-response question may test evaluation, but in this case each component will have slightly less evaluation contained in it. Be willing to use the various cases you have read about to illustrate the points you are making. These can be extremely useful in ensuring that your answer stands out from the crowd and will allow you to go beyond the confines of the extract.

How to evaluate

There is a range of ways to evaluate. You can consider any of the four points made here, as long as they are adapted to suit the context of the question.

- **Time.** Consider the time frame being looked at. Is the data over 1 year? Could there be more information? Does the data give you only a brief snapshot? Also contrast the short-run impact of any changes you discuss with the long-run impact. Consider how long it will take for something to happen — will it take a few months for an airline to expand operations or will it take some years?
- **Size of change.** You should always consider the magnitude of any change, calculate the percentage change and then draw conclusions as to whether this is significant. For example, profits of £500 million may appear a lot, but when set against sales of £10 billion, in fact they only represent 5% of all sales and may not be as significant.
- **Likelihood.** Consider how likely something is to happen. For example, how likely is the government to renationalise the railway industry? There may be other factors to consider, like the cost of nationalisation or government failure (Unit 1).
- **Wider impact.** Consider what the effect will be on the industry or the economy. How might other firms react? For example, if a firm lowers prices to try to gain an increased share of the market, might this result in a price war?

Evaluation is a skill and like all skills, it can be developed through practice. As you read an article or watch a news item, ask yourself these questions and discuss them with your friends. Eventually evaluation will be second nature.

The examinations are an opportunity for you to show the examiners what you know. Don't miss out on the opportunity to draw diagrams, give examples and define key terms. You don't need to get everything correct to be awarded an A or A* grade. If you have prepared well and stuck to your timing, you will give yourself a good chance of doing well in your economics examination.

Content Guidance

Unit 3: Business Economics and Economic Efficiency can be extremely theoretical. It is essential that you learn the diagrams and are comfortable with manipulating the various curves that are presented and used in this guide.

This Content Guidance is focused on essential information you need for the exam. It is not a substitute for your class notes but a support, and should be used alongside what you have done in class.

The information is organised under the following headings:
- Firms
- Costs and revenues
- Motives of the firm
- Theory of the firm
- Competition policy

Firms

A 'firm' can be described as the basic entity selling goods and services in an economy. It can be a sole trader, partnership or a larger company. 'Industry' is the term used to describe a collection of firms operating in the same line of business.

Why do firms grow?

Firms grow for a variety of reasons. They may decide to grow larger to:
- **Increase market share** — and become the dominant firm in a particular industry.
- **Benefit from greater profits** — a firm aims to maximise profits and may be able to achieve this through expansion.
- **Increase sales** — through larger brand recognition and more sales outlets.
- **Increase economies of scale** — in other words, the firm is able to exploit their increased size and lower long-run average cost (*LRAC*). Furthermore, by driving down *LRAC* and approaching the minimum point on the *LRAC* curve, the firm is moving closer to productive efficiency.
- **Gain power** — so as to prevent potential takeovers by larger predator businesses.

How do firms grow?

Firms can grow by expanding the scale of their operations and gaining market share. This is known as internal growth. They can also grow through takeovers, of which there are a number of different types.

Horizontal takeover

This is a merger between two firms at the same stage of production, for example Bank Santander and Alliance & Leicester in July 2008 and Anheuser Busch and Interbrew (both brewers) in July 2008.

Vertical takeover

This is a merger between firms at different stages of the productive process within an industry. This can be:
- **Forward:** at the next stage of the production process e.g. American Apparel, which designs, manufactures and sells its products, owning design, manufacture and retail components.
- **Backward:** at the previous stage of the production process e.g. Best Buy, an electronics retailer buying Napster, an online music retailer.
- **Conglomerate:** where there is a merger between firms in entirely unrelated industries. This may be done to achieve greater spread of risk, as is the case with Unilever, which has acquired over 900 brands over the years in food production, beauty products and household goods.

Why do some firms remain small?

While there are clear advantages to be gained from growth, it is obvious that some firms remain small for a number of reasons.

Barriers to entry

These barriers to growth or even entry into an industry can take the form of legal barriers or overt barriers.

Legal barriers include the need to have a permit to operate, as do accountancy and law firms, or the need to have a licence from the government, as in the case of a commercial radio station.

Overt barriers are those imposed by businesses currently operational in the industry. This could be through branding, a new advertising campaign to re-establish brand recognition or lowering prices to just above average cost to make it unprofitable to enter the industry (limit pricing). If prices are lowered below average cost to prevent incumbents from expanding (predatory pricing), then this can be considered anti-competitive. If this can be proven, firms can be fined.

Sunk costs are costs which firms will not be able to recover on exit. This means that they will need to factor these in when considering entering a market. Markets which are not contestable will have high sunk costs such as advertising, the cost of which a firm may not recover once it has been spent. Firms may have managed to erect high barriers to entry; for example, by establishing brand loyalty, which will need a large and successful advertising campaign to overcome.

Niche-market businesses

If a firm serves a niche market which will not support expansion, there is little scope for growth; for instance, manufacturers of cricket bats or a local grocery store.

Lack of expertise

The owner of the firm may lack the knowledge or expertise to expand. This may also mean they lack access to the necessary funds to expand.

Optimum efficiency has been achieved

In this instance, a firm has already exploited economies of scale and is operating at the most productively efficient point. Any further increase would result in inefficiencies and an increase in average cost. Take, for example, the case of a family-run restaurant. Any expansion, such as opening another restaurant, may require the hiring of a manager and the training of a chef. The loss of personal managerial control may result in increased cost and eventually losses.

Benefits of remaining small

Small firms are able to access additional training grants and government financial support. For example, firms with profits of less than £10 000 are not liable for corporation tax and firms with sales of less than £60 000 are not liable for value-added tax in the UK.

content guidance

Lack of motivation

Expansion may result in increased rewards but perhaps the opportunity cost in terms of lost leisure may be too much for a sole trader, and therefore they remain small; in other words they lack the motivation to expand.

Avoid attention from potential buyers

The growth of the firm and its increased profits may result in unwanted overtures from larger firms wishing to buy out the sole trader. It is therefore an advantage to remain small and avoid attention.

Why do some firms break up?

Some firms may grow too large and experience diseconomies of scale. As a result of the growth of output, the business and managers may lose focus and control over day-to-day management of the firm and therefore long-run average costs increase. To avoid this, or to reduce the impact of diseconomies of scale, a firm may decide to break up — in other words, to demerge. This may then create a number of smaller firms, all able to concentrate on their specialist area and maximise their own economies of scale.

Firms that have demerged include British Gas, which eventually formed three separate companies with different boards and management structures, all focusing on distinct aspects of the business. These were Centrica (focused on selling gas), Lattice Group (focused on transportation of gas — this has since merged with National Grid) and BG (which specialises in the production of gas).

Essentials for the examination

- Know why some firms will grow — be able to discuss the advantages of growth.
- Know how firms grow — be able to identify whether a merger between two firms is vertical, horizontal or conglomerate.
- Know why some firms remain small.
- Understand and be able to apply a number of barriers to entry to a variety of industries.
- Know why some firms may decide to become smaller through the process of demerger.

Costs and revenues

A good understanding of costs and revenues is essential to be able to appreciate fully the various market structures and to be able to answer the supported multiple-choice section with confidence.

Costs

Understanding costs allows firms to work out how efficient they are in terms of production. There are two types of cost:

- **Total fixed costs.** These costs do not vary with output. Fixed costs can only apply when at least one factor of production (land, labour, capital and entrepreneurship) is fixed. This will only be the case in the short run. For example, an out-of-town supermarket has a fixed supply of available land in the short term. In the future, the supermarket may be able to buy more land adjacent to the site, showing that in the long run, all factors of production are variable.
- **Total variable costs.** These costs do vary with output and can occur both in the short run and long run. An example may be a firm's electricity costs, which will increase as the firm is open for longer hours and more days.

Taken together, total fixed costs and total variable costs are known as **total costs**.

It is essential that you learn the formulae below, as they will help when answering supported multiple-choice questions.

Firms are interested in their total costs but are more interested in average costs. This is the cost per unit of production and gives a much more accurate picture of the firm's position.

Efficiency

- Productive efficiency occurs at the bottom of the average cost curve. It is the lowest unit cost — in other words, the firm is producing as much as possible using the fewest inputs.
- Allocative efficiency occurs when a firm produces a mix of goods using scarce resources in such a way as to meet the demands of consumers. Firms will charge a price equal to the marginal cost of manufacturing the good.

Average costs
Average fixed cost
Average fixed cost (*AFC*) is calculated as follows:

$$\frac{\text{Fixed costs}}{\text{Output}}$$

For example, if a firm's fixed costs are £1000 and output is 100, *AFC* is calculated as follows:

$$AFC = \frac{£1000}{100} = £10 \text{ per unit of output}$$

As output increases, AFC will always continue to fall, because the fixed cost is being spread across a greater output. If we assume fixed costs are £1000 and increase the output from 10 to 1000, we can see how AFC reduces:

$$AFC = \frac{£1000}{10} = £100$$

$$AFC = \frac{£1000}{100} = £10$$

$$AFC = \frac{£1000}{1000} = £1$$

Average variable cost

Average variable cost (AVC) is calculated as follows:

$$\frac{\text{Variable costs}}{\text{Output}}$$

For example, if a firm's total variable cost is £5000 and it produces 100 units, AVC is calculated as follows:

$$AVC = \frac{£5000}{100} = £50 \text{ per unit of output}$$

Therefore, based on the example above, at an output of 100, the average total cost (ATC) is equal to the AFC and AVC, in other words £10 + £50 = £60.

Marginal cost

Marginal cost (MC) can be defined as the change in total cost as a result of an additional unit of output produced.

$$\text{Marginal cost} = \frac{\text{change in total cost}}{\text{change in output}} \quad \text{or} \quad \frac{\Delta TC}{\Delta Q}$$

Output	Total cost	Marginal cost $\left(\frac{\Delta TC}{\Delta Q}\right)$
0	£100	—
1	£119	£19
2	£135	£16
3	£149	£14

You can see that, as output increases from zero to one, the total cost rises by £19. This is the marginal cost.

Marginal cost always goes through the minimum point of the average variable cost and average total cost curves (as in Figure 1 below).

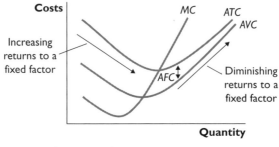

Figure 1 Short-run average costs

Note that the gap between the average total and the average variable cost is always diminishing. This is because the average fixed cost is always getting smaller.

The average total cost and average variable cost curves slope downwards because of increasing returns to a fixed factor. In other words, as greater inputs are added to a fixed factor such as a shop or factory floor, the firm will increase output at a faster rate and therefore average costs will fall. However, beyond the lowest point of the ATC and AVC, the firm begins to experience diminishing returns to a fixed factor and therefore, as additional factors of production are added to a fixed factor, they start to overcrowd each other and the ATC and AVC start to increase.

Economies and diseconomies of scale

In the long run, all costs are variable and therefore the U-shaped average cost curve can be explained by economies and diseconomies of scale.

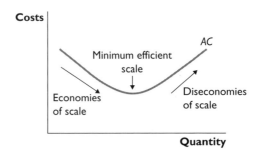

Figure 2 Economies and diseconomies of scale

Economies of scale

It is important that, as part of your preparation for the examination, you learn a number of types of economies of scale, so that you can apply these to different scenarios.

Internal economies of scale

Internal economies of scale can be defined as a fall in long-run average cost associated with an increase in output for an individual firm.

Examples of economies of scale include:

- **Financial economies.** As a firm grows in size, it is better able to access loans at low cost. Banks will be more willing to lend, as there is less risk associated with the transaction.
- **Risk-bearing economies.** As the firm expands, it is better able to develop a range of products and a wider customer base to spread risk and minimise the impact of any downturn.
- **Marketing economies.** As a firm expands its product range, it is able to use any central brand marketing to advertise the range at little extra cost and therefore spread this across a wider range of goods and lower long-run average cost. For example, if Mars advertises their chocolate bars, they are also indirectly advertising their ice cream with no additional cost by developing brand awareness.
- **Managerial economies.** As a firm expands, it is in a position to employ specialist managers in finance, sales, operations and so on, and therefore increase productivity and lower long-run average costs.
- **Increased dimensions.** A haulage company, for example, is able to expand the quantities they carry by doubling the dimensions and therefore the costs, but in consequence they increase the volume eight-fold (see Figure 3).

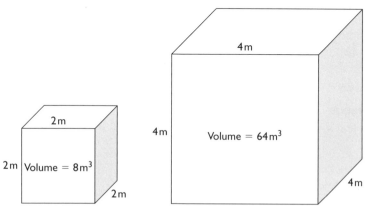

Figure 3 Increased dimensions

External economies of scale

Internal economies of scale occur when an individual firm expands, whereas external economies of scale have an impact on the entire industry and therefore lower the long-run average cost curve, as illustrated in Figure 4.

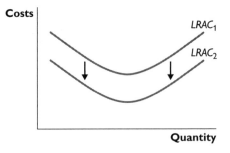

Figure 4 External economies of scale

An industry may benefit as a result of innovations produced by other firms and therefore all firms will see their average cost of production fall.

Retailers located close to each other are able to benefit from the development of new roads and transport links and so lower the long-run average costs of all the firms.

A group of small businesses is able to share administrative and secretarial facilities and therefore lower long-run costs per unit.

Diseconomies of scale

A firm may experience diseconomies of scale if it grows too large and moves beyond its minimum efficient scale. Diseconomies of scale may result from a breakdown in communication or other managerial difficulties and will result in long-run average costs increasing as output increases. This may occur when a firm merges with another or when a firm grows internally and management lacks the experience necessary to maintain managerial focus and control.

Revenues

Total revenue

Total revenue is the same as the turnover of the firm. It can be calculated as:

$$\text{Price} \times \text{Quantity}$$

Average revenue

Firms are also interested in the average revenue (AR), or revenue per unit. This can be calculated:

$$AR = \frac{\text{Total revenue}}{\text{Quantity}}$$

Marginal revenue

Equally important, especially when calculating profit maximisation, is marginal revenue. This is the revenue associated with each additional unit sold, i.e. the change in total revenue from selling one more unit.

Output	Total revenue	Marginal revenue
10	63	–
11	75	12
12	86	11

Both average revenue and marginal revenue tend to be downward sloping, as in Figure 5 (unless the firm is operating under conditions of perfect competition), and reflect the downward-sloping demand curve and the need for firms to lower prices to increase sales.

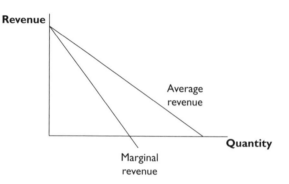

Figure 5 Average and marginal revenue

Therefore, the average revenue curve is also the firm's demand curve. This can be calculated by:

$$\text{Average revenue} = \frac{P \times Q}{Q}$$

In this equation, quantity can be cancelled out:

$$\frac{P \times \cancel{Q}}{\cancel{Q}}$$

Therefore AR can be said to be equal to P.

Essentials for the examination

- Know how to distinguish between the short run and long run.
- Be able to distinguish and explain what is meant by a fixed and variable cost.
- Know how to calculate average and marginal costs.
- Understand the relationship between average and marginal costs.
- Be able to draw and manipulate average and marginal costs.
- Be able to define accurately economies of scale and discuss a few economies of scale. In particular, be able to apply them to a specific industry or firm.

- Be able to calculate average and marginal revenue.
- Understand the relationship between average and marginal revenue and be able to draw this.

Motives of the firm

Firms are assumed to be profit maximisers, but sometimes they may opt to satisfy different objectives such as revenue maximisation and sales maximisation.

Profit maximisation

Profit maximisation occurs at the output level where super-normal profits are at their greatest (or losses are at their lowest). This occurs where marginal cost is equal to marginal revenue, but while this is a necessary condition, it is not sufficient. Marginal cost must also be rising.

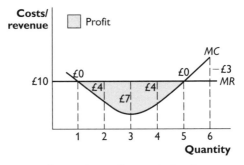

Figure 6 Profit maximisation

In Figure 6, at an output of one, marginal profit is zero; in other words, there is no profit from the last unit sold. The difference between this output and the next time we have a marginal profit of zero (five units sold) is that at an output of five the firm is maximising its profits. This is because we can see each unit sold between one and five is adding to total profit. The figures from Figure 6 are converted into a table below.

Output	Marginal revenue	Marginal cost	Marginal profit	Total profit
1	£10	£10	£0	£0
2	£10	£6	£4	£4
3	£10	£3	£7	£11
4	£10	£6	£4	£15
5	£10	£10	£0	£15
6	£10	£13	−£3	£12

When the fifth unit is sold, marginal cost equals marginal revenue, and as we know that marginal cost is rising, then the next unit sold (the sixth) will cause marginal cost to rise above marginal revenue. In other words, the sixth unit sold results in a marginal loss of £3 and therefore a fall in total profit from the peak of £15 to £12.

Therefore, firms will seek to equate marginal cost with marginal revenue to maximise profits.

When evaluating profit maximisation, consider whether the local pub or coffee shop knows the marginal cost of a pint of beer or a cup of coffee. Furthermore, what would they do if they knew that level of output? Would they stop selling because the next item would result in a fall in total profit? Some firms, then, look to other objectives.

Revenue maximisation

Revenue maximisation occurs when a firm seeks to make as much revenue as possible. Firms are therefore willing to sell products until the last unit sold adds nothing to total revenue, knowing that the next unit sold will reduce revenue. This can be illustrated by the diagram in Figure 7.

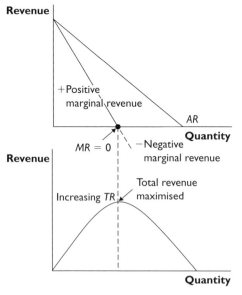

Figure 7 Revenue maximisation where **MR = 0**

Figure 7 shows that, as the firm expands output, the marginal revenue declines (remember that marginal revenue is the addition to total revenue from one more unit sold). However, while marginal revenue is positive, it continues to add to total revenue; it is only when it passes zero and becomes negative that total revenue starts to decline.

Sales maximisation

Sales maximisation occurs when a firm attempts to sell as much as it can without making a loss. This occurs where average cost equals average revenue.

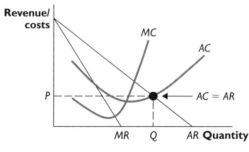

Figure 8 Sales maximisation where **AC = AR**

Firms may embark on revenue or sales maximisation in an effort to gain market share or drive a rival out of the industry.

Governments, on the other hand, may seek to ensure that their firms operate at the allocatively efficient point (Figure 9). This is where price equals marginal cost. In other words, the price paid for a good is equal to the cost of the factors of production used to manufacture the last unit.

In this case, firms are not profit maximising and so it is unlikely that a private firm will decide to price at this level.

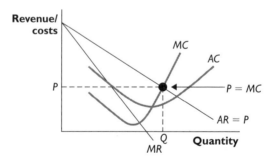

Figure 9 Allocative efficiency where **P = MC**

Pricing strategies

In addition to the motives of the firm discussed so far, firms can decide to adopt a number of strategies designed to gain market share.

- **Predatory pricing:** pricing at a level low enough to drive out firms currently in the industry by reducing profitability.
- **Limit pricing:** pricing at a level low enough to limit profits, which has the effect of discouraging new entrants from joining the industry.

In the short run, both limit and predatory pricing will benefit the consumer by providing them with low prices. However, when the firm has managed to drive rival firms out of the industry and gained monopoly power, it will be able to raise prices, reducing the consumer surplus and exploiting the consumer.

Non-pricing strategies

As an alternative to limit pricing and predatory pricing, firms may embark on non-price competition. This is particularly relevant when firms sell goods which cannot be discounted heavily or where some form of collusion takes place.

This non-price competition includes:
- advertising
- branding
- packaging
- after care/customer service/warranties
- product development and innovation
- product placement — the type of retail outlet in which the good is sold

Behavioural motives of the firm

Firms and their managers are generally expected to behave rationally and therefore to profit maximise. However, there may be occasions when managers or owners will follow other goals.

For example, they may decide to maximise their own personal welfare or ego by growing the business or taking over a rival firm, or to maximise their short-term bonus while taking significant risks with the future viability of the business.

Managers may decide to profit satisfice — in other words, to achieve the minimum level of profit required by the owners but then devote time to achieving other goals, such as spending time on the golf course. This type of behaviour sees profit not as a goal to be pursued, but rather a minimum target that needs to be obtained before other goals can be pursued.

Essentials for the examination
- Ensure you are able to show on a diagram where a firm seeks to profit maximise (i.e. $MC = MR$); revenue maximise (i.e. $MR = 0$) and sales maximise (i.e. $AC = AR$).
- Remember the difference between predatory and limit pricing.
- Be willing to offer alternatives to pricing policies.

Theory of the firm

In this section the various market structures under which firms operate will be examined. These form the main part of this module.

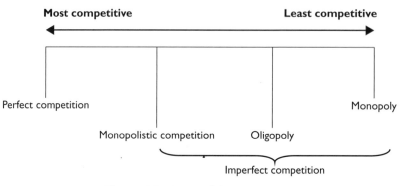

Figure 10 Competition spectrum

The characteristics of each model are essential in identifying which market structure is being considered. They should be used whenever you are asked a question about a firm to help justify your answer.

Summary of the key characteristics of market structures

	Perfect competition	Monopolistic competition	Oligopoly	Monopoly
Number of firms	Many small firms	Many small firms	A few large firms dominate	One
Type of product	Homogenous	Similar	Similar	Unique
Knowledge	Perfect	Imperfect	Imperfect	Imperfect
Barriers to entry/exit	None	Low	High	High
Price-setting powers	Price taker	Price setter to a limited extent	Some price setting powers	Price setter

When considering market structure, it is always useful to consider how many firms dominate the market. In highly concentrated markets few firms dominate; for example, the mobile phone industry or the UK banking sector.

The **concentration ratio** can be defined as the market share controlled by the 'n' largest firms. For example, the four-firm concentration ratio is the market share of an industry controlled by the four largest firms. An oligopoly would be highly concentrated and a monopolistically competitive market would have a low concentration ratio.

Perfect competition

Characteristics

Characteristics of perfect competition

Number of firms	Many small firms
Type of product	Homogenous (exactly the same)
Knowledge	Perfect knowledge — this doesn't mean the firm knows everything about rival firms' price and output decisions. Rather, it means the firm has access to this information, including the latest technology and techniques and information on who makes super-normal profits
Barriers to entry/exit	None
Price setting powers	None — perfectly competitive firms take the price set by the market. They are known as **price takers** (see Figure 11)

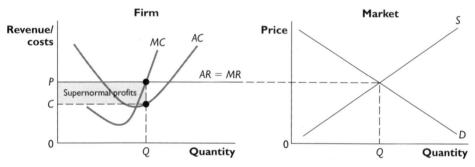

Figure 11 Short-run supernormal profits in perfect competition

In this diagram, the firm is taking the industry- or market-determined price (P). This is above the firm's average cost at the output level, which corresponds to the profit-maximising output of $MC = MR$. Therefore, the firm is making supernormal profits, as indicated on the diagram.

From the diagram we can see that the firm is operating in the short run. Perfectly competitive firms cannot maintain supernormal profits in the long run, because rival firms will see that these supernormal profits are being made (because of perfect knowledge) and enter the industry (no barriers to entry) and therefore the market-supply curve shifts to the right and the price falls (see Figure 12), until all the supernormal profits are competed away and the firms make normal profits in the long run.

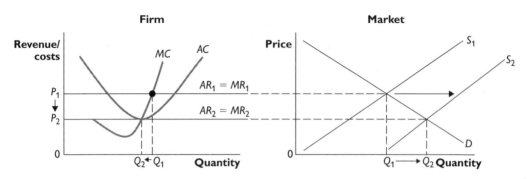

Figure 12 Competition causing prices to fall in long-run perfect competition

The diagram shows the market output increase from Q_1 to Q_2 and the firm reacts to this drop in price from P_1 to P_2 by reducing output to Q_2.

Thus, in the long run, a perfectly competitive firm will always make normal profits only, any supernormal profits having been competed away and the losses absorbed by firms leaving the industry. This is known as the **long-run equilibrium** (Figure 13).

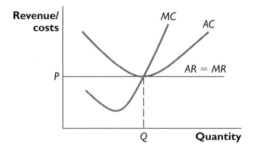

Figure 13 Long-run equilibrium in perfect competition

The shut-down point for a perfectly competitive firm occurs when the firm is not covering average variable costs in the short run. In other words, it may be feasible for a firm to make a loss in the short run, as long as it covers the cost of making the good and therefore makes a contribution to the fixed costs. This is illustrated in the table opposite by comparing the example of a firm that shuts down and has to pay its fixed costs with a firm that stays open and therefore makes a contribution to fixed costs.

Therefore, by remaining open, the firm is able to reduce its loss down to £70 000 and it makes a contribution of £30 000 towards fixed costs.

The supply curve of a perfectly competitive firm operating in the short run is therefore the marginal cost curve above the average variable cost. At this level of output, when the marginal revenue crosses the marginal cost, the firm will remain open, as it makes a contribution toward fixed costs (see Figure 14).

Firm closing	Firm remaining open
Quantity produced = 0	Quantity produced = 10 000
Fixed costs = £100 000	Fixed costs = £100 000
Loss = **£100 000**	Price per unit = £10 (average revenue)
	Therefore, total revenue $(P \times Q)$ = £10 × 10 000 = £100 000
	Variable cost per unit (AVC) = £7
	Total variable costs, i.e. $AVC \times Q$ = £7 × 10 000 = £70 000
	The total cost is made up of fixed costs and variable costs, i.e. £100 000 + £70 000 = £170 000
	Total revenue = £100 000 − total cost = £170 000
	Thus the loss by staying open is **£70 000**, which makes a contribution to fixed costs

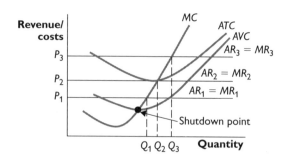

Figure 14 Supply curve for a perfectly competitive firm

The firm will be indifferent as to whether it stays open at the shutdown point. It will operate at Q_1, Q_2 or Q_3, in other words, when the marginal cost is above the average variable cost, and it will shut down if it cannot cover average variable costs.

Monopolistic competition

Characteristics

Monopolistically competitive firms exhibit many of the characteristics of firms operating under conditions of perfect competition. However, they are able to set price to a limited extent during the short run because the products they produce are not exactly the same and customers will, therefore, have some brand loyalty. Hence, this market structure combines elements of both perfect competition and monopoly. Examples include restaurants, hairdressers and florists.

Characteristics of monopolistic competition

Number of firms	Many small firms
Type of product	Similar goods, slightly differentiated
Knowledge	Imperfect knowledge about rival firms' price and output decisions but firms will be able to identify when supernormal profits are being made
Barriers to entry/exit	Low
Price-setting powers	Firms can price set to an extent because they will produce goods which are slightly different from rival firms' goods

In the short run, a monopolistically competitive firm can make supernormal profits as illustrated in Figure 15. Like all other imperfectly competitive firms, a monopolistically competitive firm need not operate at the productively or allocatively efficient levels of output.

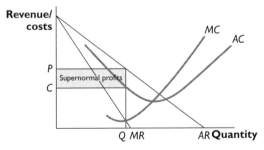

Figure 15 Supernormal profits in short-run monopolistic competition

However, in the same way that a perfectly competitive firm cannot maintain supernormal profits in the long run, a monopolistically competitive firm cannot maintain supernormal profits in the long run due to the low barriers to entry that allow firms to enter the market and compete profits away. It is for that reason that the long-run

32

position for a monopolistically competitive firm is in the equilibrium as depicted in Figure 16.

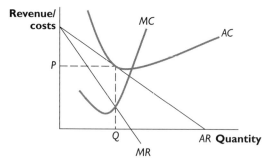

Figure 16 Long-run equilibrium in monopolistic competition

Oligopoly

Characteristics

Oligopoly is characterised by the interdependent nature of the firms operating within this market structure. The interdependent nature of this structure is largely due to the fact that a few firms dominate the market and sell similar, yet branded, goods. This sort of market structure typically plays host to collusive behaviour among the main firms. Typical examples of oligopolies include the brewing industry, pharmaceuticals, food and confectionery manufacturers and petrol retail stores.

Characteristics of oligopoly

Number of firms	A few large firms dominate and can coexist with many small firms
Type of product	Similar goods but branded
Knowledge	Imperfect knowledge about rival firms' price and output decisions
Barriers to entry/exit	High
Price-setting powers	Oligopolies can price set but may decide to agree price-fixing deals with rivals to avoid price competition

Competition in oligopolies

With only a few firms dominating an industry (i.e. there is a high concentration ratio), firms will tend to avoid price competition. This happens because if one firm were to lower prices, others would follow and although they may gain some additional sales, this would be at the cost of lost revenue from the price war that would ensue.

Therefore an oligopoly is also characterised by non-price competition; in other words, the firms compete through:

- advertising
- branding
- product quality/innovation
- packaging
- free gifts
- store loyalty cards e.g. Sainsbury's Nectar or Tesco's Clubcard

Collusion in oligopolies

Oligopoly is often associated with collusion and price-fixing deals because firms tend to produce similar goods. To show greater levels of collusion, an industry should exhibit certain additional characteristics:

- **Similar costs** — to allow for similar pricing
- **Few firms** — the fewer the number of firms, the easier it is to share information between one another
- **High barriers to entry** — these allow the firms to make supernormal profits in the long run and prevent new firms from entering the industry
- **Low levels of regulation** — collusion is illegal but if the regulators can be easily outwitted or if fines are low, collusive practices are more likely

A number of firms have been fined for collusive behaviour in recent years. These include: British Airways, for fixing the price of fuel surcharges along with Virgin Atlantic; LG Electronics and Sharp Corporation, who were fined by US anti-trust regulators for price fixing liquid crystal displays; and Manchester United Football Club and several sportswear forms, who were found guilty of price fixing football shirts.

However, as was seen in the example of British Airways and Virgin Atlantic, there is always a temptation to break an agreement either to maximise a firm's sales by lowering prices and catching a rival unaware or, as in the case of Virgin Atlantic, to gain immunity from prosecution.

This can be illustrated in a simple game theory 2×2 matrix illustrated in Figure 17.

Let us assume that there are two firms, called Adrian and Juju, in an industry. It is clear that if Adrian and Juju collude, they will be able to make profits of £100 million each by setting prices at a high level (Box A). However, they each know that they can increase their individual profits by lowering prices and breaking any collusive agreement, so obtaining £120 million (Boxes B and C). As a result of neither firm trusting the other, they will both adopt the low-price strategy and end up with £80 million (Box D), which is a worse outcome than if they had colluded and set a high price. This suggests that due to a lack of trust between firms any collusive agreement is likely to be broken.

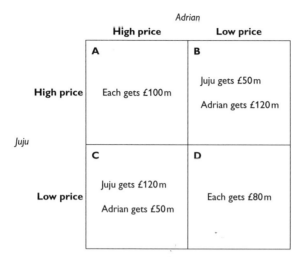

Figure 17 Game theory 2 × 2 matrix

Monopoly

Characteristics

Monopoly is the least competitive market structure. Only one firm operates and as a consequence, it is able to set prices and output and to maximise profits.

Characteristics of monopoly

Number of firms	One
Type of product	Unique
Knowledge	Imperfect knowledge. Potential rival firms will not know the incumbent firms' pricing and output strategy
Barriers to entry/exit	High
Price-setting powers	Price setter

As a result of high barriers to entry, monopolists can set high prices to maximise profits without fear that another firm could enter the industry. It is for this reason that many governments will intervene to prevent the development of monopolies and ensure that competition is maintained in some form. Monopolies are also often accused of being lazy and less inclined to innovate and develop new products because they have no need to maintain an edge over competitors.

Monopolists will operate on the elastic part of their demand curve and seek to maximise profits, therefore reducing consumer surplus. Unlike a perfectly competitive firm, monopolists will also not operate at the allocatively efficient point ($P = MC$) or the productively efficient point (i.e. the lowest point on the average cost curve).

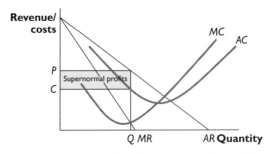

Figure 18 Supernormal profits in a monopoly market structure

Comparing monopoly with perfect competition

	Monopoly	Perfect competition
Profit maximisers	Yes	Yes
Allocatively efficient	No	Yes
Productively efficient	No	Yes
Price	Prices are higher under monopoly compared to perfect competition	Prices are lower under perfect competition compared to monopoly
Quantity	Quantity is lower under monopoly compared to perfect competition	Quantity is higher under perfect competition compared to monopoly

Advantages and disadvantages of monopoly

Disadvantages of monopoly power	Advantages of monopoly power
Supernormal profit means: • Less incentive to be efficient and to develop new products • The existence of resources to protect market dominance by raising barriers to entry	Supernormal profit means: • Finance for investment to maintain competitive edge • Firms can also create reserves to overcome short-term difficulties, giving stability to employment • Funds for research and development
Monopoly power means: • Higher prices and lower output for domestic consumers	Monopoly power means: • Firms will have the financial power to match large overseas competitors
Monopolies may waste resources by undertaking cross-subsidisation, using profits from one sector to finance losses in another sector.	Cross-subsidisation may lead to an increased range of goods or services available to the consumer, for example the provision of services that are loss-making but provide an external benefit e.g. rural bus services.

Disadvantages of monopoly power	Advantages of monopoly power
Monopolists may undertake price discrimination to raise producer surplus and reduce consumer surplus.	Price discrimination may raise the firm's total revenue to a point which allows the survival of a product or service.
Monopolists do not produce at the most productively efficient point of output (i.e. at the lowest point of the average cost curve).	Monopolists may be able to take advantage of economies of scale, which means that average costs may be lower than those of a competitive firm at its most efficient position. This is especially the case when there is a natural monopoly.
Monopolists can be complacent and develop inefficiencies.	There are few permanent monopolies and the supernormal profit opportunities act as an incentive for rival firms to break down the monopoly through a process of creative destruction, i.e. breaking the monopoly by product development and innovation, and therefore bypassing any barriers to entry.
Monopolies may lead to a misallocation of resources by setting prices above marginal cost, so that price is above the opportunity cost of providing the good, i.e. price $\neq$ marginal cost.	Monopolists can avoid undesirable duplication of services.

Price discrimination

Monopolists can use high barriers to entry in order to engage in price discrimination. This occurs when a firm sells the same product to two different markets with differing elasticities at different prices. This allows the monopolist to increase profits and to reduce consumer surplus (Unit 1 synoptic point).

To embark on price discrimination a firm must fulfil three conditions:
- Possess high barriers to entry and a degree of monopoly power.
- Identify at least two separate markets with differing elasticities.
- Keep these markets separate at a cost that is lower than the gain in profits. This is to prevent resale (arbitrage) between the two markets.

There are three types of price discrimination.

First-degree price discrimination

This type of price discrimination is primarily theoretical because it requires the seller of a good or service to know the absolute maximum price that every consumer is willing to pay. By knowing the maximum price each person is willing to pay, the seller is able to absorb the entire market surplus, thus taking the entire consumer surplus from the consumer and transforming it into revenues.

First-degree price discrimination is not undesirable as the market is still entirely efficient and there is no deadweight loss to society. However, it is the complete opposite of a perfectly competitive market. In a perfectly competitive market, the consumers receive the bulk of the surplus. In a market with first-degree price discrimination, the seller captures the entire consumer surplus.

The closest example of this type of price discrimination is seen in a bidding process such as that on eBay, where a consumer can offer as high a price as they are willing to pay.

Second-degree price discrimination

This type of price discrimination is based on the amount sold, with bulk-buying being a typical example. This is often seen in industrial processes, where a firm can be rewarded for the quantity of a product that it buys.

Third-degree price discrimination

This can be based on regional, age or time differences. Examples of this type of price discrimination include the sale of child and adult railway tickets and the sale of peak and off-peak telephone, electricity and gas services.

Third-degree price discrimination is the most common type of price discrimination and is illustrated in Figure 19. The firm splits the market into elastic and inelastic demand, selling the output at different prices to the two markets and keeping these separate.

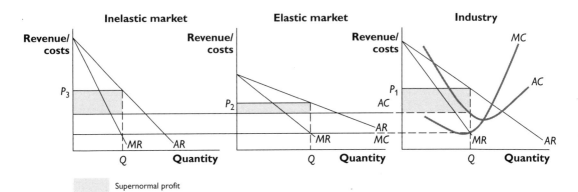

Figure 19 Third-degree price discrimination

Natural monopoly

A natural monopoly exists when an industry can only support one firm. This is typical of an industry which has high sunk costs and requires large levels of output to exploit economies of scale.

The introduction of competition, perhaps by some government agency, will not be possible in the long run, as neither of the competing firms is able to obtain sufficient market share to ensure that it is best able to exploit economies of scale.

Natural monopolies exist in the supply of water, gas and electricity, where there are high start up and infrastructure costs. The costs of establishing a competing firm will outweigh any economic or social benefit that may materialise. This is illustrated in Figure 20, where it is clear that the firm operates at the profit maximising point when it reaches an output of 1 million. Should the market be opened to competition and both firms take an equal share of the market, i.e. 500 000, they will each make a loss. If one of the firms gained a greater market share then it may be able to survive, but this will be at the expense of the other firm that will eventually fail, returning the industry back to having only one firm.

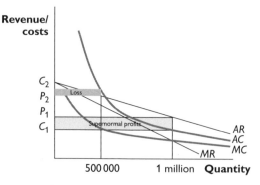

Figure 20 Natural monopoly

Contestable markets

A contestable market exists when a market is said to have low sunk costs and therefore low barriers to entry and exit. This will mean new firms can quickly enter an industry when they see supernormal profits being made and exploit these before leaving the industry. These are referred to as 'hit and run' profits.

In recent years, as a result of the ability to lease aeroplanes, the airline industry has become more contestable, with the growth of low-cost airlines as rivals to the more established national carriers.

Monopsony

A monopsony occurs when many sellers face only one buyer. For example, if an individual wishes to work in emergency medicine in the UK, then the sole buyer of such employees is the National Health Service. A number of firms could act together to form a single buyer. In the supermarket industry, for example, the major retailers may join together to exploit the sellers and ensure that the supermarkets are able to get the best possible price for their goods.

This sort of power may allow a firm to exploit its suppliers in the knowledge that the supplier has few options beyond selling to the sole buyer. This can mean that cheaper prices are passed on to the consumer, but this may be at the expense of the supplier of the goods.

Essentials for the examination

- Learn and understand all the diagrams for perfect competition and imperfect competition.
- Know the characteristics of the various market structures and be willing to use them to support a discussion of why a particular industry may resemble one of the market structures discussed so far.
- Understand the simple game theory matrix.
- Know the difference between first-degree, second-degree and third-degree price discrimination.
- Know the advantages and disadvantages of monopoly.
- Know the definition of a contestable market.
- Be able to determine whether a firm is a natural monopoly and the characteristics of this sort of industry.
- Know what is meant by monopsony and how a firm can use such a position to achieve maximum benefit.

Competition policy

The Competition Commission conducts inquiries into mergers between firms in response to requests from the Office of Fair Trading (OFT). Usually this will take place if the merger of two firms will result in a market share greater than 25% or if it meets the 'turnover test' of a combined turnover of £70 million or more. This market share may allow a firm to exhibit the characteristics of a monopoly and dominate the market. Since the introduction of the Enterprise Act of 2002, there have been new regulations for assessing whether a merger should be allowed to proceed. The commission determines whether a merger will impact adversely on competition. In other words, if it 'prevents, restricts or distorts competition', then the merger is likely to be blocked.

Methods of regulation

Since privatisation of the state-owned monopolies such as British Telecom, British Gas and the electricity and water industries in the 1980s and early 1990s, the government has appointed a regulator as a surrogate to competition to set price and maintain quality. Since competition has been established in the telecoms, gas and electricity industries, the only previously state-owned industry still to have prices set by the regulator is water.

Price capping

RPI – X

This takes the retail price index (RPI — a measure of inflation that you will have come across in Unit 2) and subtracts a factor 'X' determined by the regulator. 'X' represents the efficiency gains that the regulator has determined can reasonably be achieved by the firm in question. This method was at one time used to regulate British Gas and British Telecom.

RPI + K

This method uses the RPI and allows the addition of the 'K' factor which accounts for the additional capital spending that a firm has agreed with the regulator is necessary. This is used by the water regulator to determine the price for each of the regional water companies. The 'K' factor is different for each of the water companies, depending on how much they are required to spend to maintain and improve their quality of service.

The advantage of this method is that it allows a firm to keep any profits it makes through instigating greater efficiency gains than the regulator has calculated are reasonable. In addition, because the 'X' or 'K' factor are usually in place for 5 years, firms are able to plan ahead and know that they will not be unduly penalised for making further efficiency gains.

However, this method can be criticised. If the regulator underestimates the efficiency gains a firm can be expected to make, then firms can produce what appear to be excessive profits, although often these profits are used to invest in areas outside the regulator's remit and therefore generate even greater profits in the future. There have been suggestions in the past that the regulator and the regulated industry have built up a close relationship, resulting in the regulator being less strict on the firms under its control. This close relationship is referred to as **regulator capture**.

Rate of return

This method of regulation was used originally in the USA before price capping was adopted there.

This method allows a firm to make a certain level of profit based on their capital before the remainder of the profit is taxed at 100%. Unlike the price-capping system, this means that there is no incentive to make efficiency gains that increase profits. Firms are not rewarded for their success; on the contrary they are penalised for it and instead encouraged to make a limited profit. In addition, firms are encouraged to overstate the value of their capital to ensure that they can increase the rate of return on their investment, in effect increasing their profits.

Performance targets

The regulator can also set performance targets that it will then monitor. These may be based on improvements in the quality of service or reductions in the number of customer complaints. This may be supported by a system of fines, should the firm fail to meet the performance targets or rewards, should the firm meet them. This has been used by the regulator to monitor the performance of the train-operating companies in the UK and to help determine future price increases.

Essentials for the examination

- Understand the characteristics of a merger that may be referred to the Competition Commission by the Office of Fair Trading.
- Know the difference between RPI − X and RPI + K and be able to calculate the changes in price to the consumer.
- Understand the advantages of RPI − X and RPI + K compared to other methods of regulation, such as rate of return.

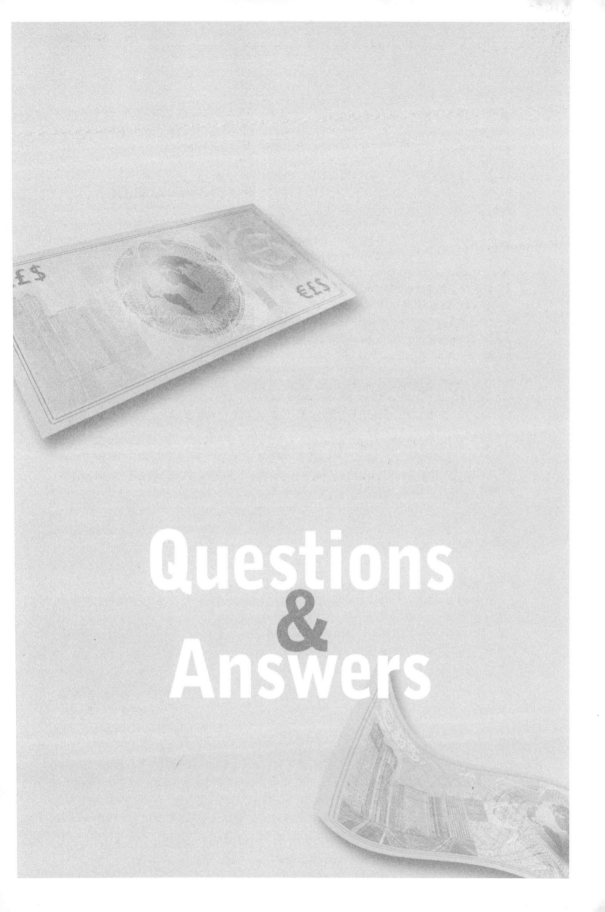

Questions
&
Answers

In the examination candidates will have to do eight supported multiple-choice questions and one data-response question from a choice of two.

In this section there are 17 supported multiple-choice questions under the chapter headings. You are strongly advised to attempt the topic-based questions only when you have completed your revision for a topic. Write out your answer to support the letter you have selected before you check the sample answers provided. Always try to imagine you are marking the answer while you are writing. Ask yourself if there are enough scoring statements to ensure full marks. Annotate diagrams or draw them to support your answer; remember to refer to them in your answer to ensure the examiner gives you full credit for your work. Define key terms and, if unsure, always knock out alternatives — you can get up to 2 marks for these knockouts. Even if you select the wrong letter, you can score a maximum of 3 marks, so never leave an answer entirely blank. At the very least, you should attempt to define the key terms in the question.

The data-response questions in this book resemble those in the examination. There will be *four* parts, with the emphasis on evaluation. Ensure you read the material and try to use diagrams wherever possible to highlight your understanding of micro-economics.

The data-response section includes student answers ranging from A to C and examiner comments explaining, where relevant, how the answer could be improved. These comments are preceded by the icon *e*.

Supported multiple-choice questions

Costs and revenues

1

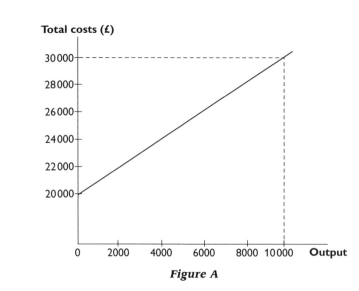

Figure A

The diagram shows the total cost for Laurence, a manufacturer of tee-shirts. At an output of 10 000 the average variable cost is:

A £30 000

B £10 000

C £1

D £2

E £3

2 Jake finds that by lowering the cost of the houses he builds from £550 000 to £500 000, annual sales rise from 10 to 11. The marginal revenue gained is:

A £50 000

B £0

C £500 000

D £100 000

E £5 500 000

3 Which of the following statements about average costs curves is correct?

A Average costs are always higher than marginal costs.

B Marginal costs are always higher than average costs.

C Average costs may be falling when marginal costs are rising.

D Average costs rise when marginal costs rise.

E Marginal costs are negative when average costs are falling.

Motives of the firm

4 Tommy has the objective of sales maximisation. He will seek to set:

A Marginal cost equal to marginal revenue

B Marginal cost equal to average revenue

C Marginal revenue equal to zero

D Average revenue equal to average cost

E Average revenue equal to zero

5 In the short run, a mobile phone supplier may continue to offer off-peak services at reduced prices, provided that the total revenue from those off-peak services covers at least:

A The total fixed costs

B The average variable costs

C The total costs

D The total variable costs

E The marginal cost

Theory of the firm: perfect competition

6 A perfectly competitive firm will be productively efficient:

A Only in the long run

B Only if it is making a loss

C Only when it makes supernormal profit

D In both the short run and the long run

E Only in the short run

7 A perfectly competitive firm is making supernormal profits. Which of the following applies to such a firm?

	Time period	Allocative efficiency	Productive efficiency
A	Long run	Yes	No
B	Long run	No	Yes
C	Short run	Yes	Yes
D	Short run	Yes	No
E	Short run	No	Yes

Theory of the firm: monopolistic competition

8 A monopolistically competitive firm operating in the long run will:
- **A** Be allocatively but not productively efficient
- **B** Make supernormal profits
- **C** Be both allocatively and productively efficient
- **D** Be productively but not allocatively efficient
- **E** Be neither productively nor allocatively efficient

9 Which of the following characteristics will a monopolistically competitive firm operating in the long run exhibit?

	Efficiency	Profit
A	Allocatively efficient	Supernormal
B	Productively efficient	Normal
C	Allocatively inefficient	Normal
D	Productively inefficient	Supernormal
E	Allocatively efficient	Normal

10 Maximillian operates a hotel in a monopolistically competitive market. The hotel is likely to:
- **A** Collude with other hotels and make supernormal profits in the long run
- **B** Offer identical services to other hotels at the same price
- **C** Operate at the lowest cost per room
- **D** Have a wider range of facilities and develop brand loyalty
- **E** Charge a price equal to the cost of providing the hotel room

Theory of the firm: oligopoly

11 A manufacturer of chocolate bars may want to engage in non-price competition rather than price competition when selling its product because:
- **A** There is the ability to create brand loyalty for chocolate bars
- **B** Chocolate bars are price elastic in demand
- **C** The marginal revenue and price of chocolates are the same
- **D** Chocolate bars are price inelastic in demand
- **E** Chocolate bars are all the same and changes in price will have no effect on other firms

12

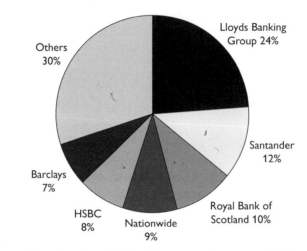

Others 30%

Lloyds Banking Group 24%

Santander 12%

Royal Bank of Scotland 10%

Nationwide 9%

HSBC 8%

Barclays 7%

Source: Adapted from British Bankers' Association — Response to the Tripartite Discussion Paper, 5 December 2007

Figure B UK retail bank deposits: market share

Which of the following is true of the UK retail banking sector?
A It is monopolistically competitive.
B It has a three-firm concentration ratio of 46%.
C It has a five-firm concentration ratio of 85%.
D It has a seven-firm concentration ratio of 100%.
E It is a monopoly.

13 Which of the following is the most likely consequence of a firm operating in an oligopoly?
A Price competition
B Normal profits in the long run
C 'Hit and run' profits
D Periods of tacit collusion
E Productive and allocative efficiency

Theory of the firm: monopoly

14 A profit-maximising monopolist switching to a policy of revenue maximisation will:
A Reduce output and raise prices
B Raise output and lower prices
C Raise output and leave prices unchanged
D Reduce output and lower prices
E Leave output unchanged and raise prices

15 C^2 is a monopoly manufacturer of high quality rugby trophies and operates at a profit maximising level of output. Which of the following must be true?
  A Marginal revenue is negative.
  B Demand is price elastic.
  C Raising output will reduce the manufacturer's total revenue.
  D Demand is price inelastic.
  E Marginal cost will be above average cost at this level of output.

Competition policy

16 In 2007, LG Electronics and Sharp Corporation were fined for price fixing LCD screens. The purpose of such a fine is to:
  A Encourage the development of agreements between LCD manufacturers
  B Reduce the costs of LCD manufacturers
  C Protect consumer interest
  D Ensure greater profits within the LCD industry
  E Increase economies of scale in the LCD industry

17 Under the Enterprise Act of 2002, the Office of Fair Trading has the power to refer any merger that leads to more than 25% of market share resting with the merged firm to the Competition Commission for investigation. The investigation is likely to recommend the merger is not allowed if it will probably result in:
  A A rise in shareholder value
  B An increase in consumer welfare
  C A reduction in market concentration
  D Greater contestability
  E A substantial reduction of competition within the market being investigated

Supported multiple-choice answers

Costs and revenues

Question 1
Correct answer C
  Total costs are £30 000. Fixed costs are £20 000 — remember at an output of 0, the only costs that the firm incurs are fixed costs. Therefore, variable costs are £10 000, so average variable costs are £1 (£10 000/output of 10 000).

Question 2
Correct answer B
  Marginal revenue is the change in total revenue from one more unit sold. Total revenue before the price cut is £550 000 × 10 = £5 500 000. Total revenue after the price cut is £500 000 × 11 = £5 500 000. As a result, there has been no change in the total revenue, and therefore no change in the marginal revenue of the business.

Question 3
Correct answer C (see Figure 1)
As marginal costs rise, a firm can still experience falling average costs. Ensure that you can draw the diagram to show this.

Motives of the firm

Question 4
Correct answer D (see Figure 8)
Sales maximisation occurs where average revenue equals average cost.

Question 5
Correct answer B (see Figure 14)
The shutdown point shown in Figure 14 is for a perfectly competitive firm; however, the principle remains the same. As long as a firm covers its average variable costs, it will continue to operate in the short run, even if it is making a loss because it is making a contribution to fixed costs.

Theory of the firm: perfect competition

Question 6
Correct answer A (see Figures 11, 12 and 13)
Productive efficiency occurs at the minimum point on the average total cost curve (where marginal cost intersects the average cost curve). In the short run, firms can make supernormal profits (see Figure 11) and losses (see Figure 12), both of which result in average costs being above the minimum point. In Figure 13, you can see the long-run equilibrium which has to occur where marginal cost intersects the average cost — in other words at the point of productively efficient output.

Question 7
Correct answer D (see Figure 11)
Perfectly competitive firms can only make supernormal profits in the short run because the low barriers to entry ensure any supernormal profits are competed away by new firms entering the industry. As in Question 8, it is clear that the firm cannot be productively efficient if it is making supernormal profits. For the firm to be allocatively efficient, it must operate where price equals marginal cost ($P = MC$); in other words, where average revenue equals marginal cost. In perfect competition, when marginal cost equals marginal revenue (profit-maximising condition), average revenue will equal marginal cost, as a result of the horizontal nature of the marginal and average revenue curves, ensuring that allocative efficiency is achieved.

Theory of the firm: monopolistic competition

Question 8
Correct answer E (see Figure 15)
Productive efficiency occurs at the lowest point on the average cost curve. Allocative efficiency occurs at $P = MC$. In Figure 15, it is clear that neither of these occurs when the firm is profit maximising.

Question 9
Correct answer C (see Figure 16)

In monopolistic competition, firms face low barriers to entry. Other firms will see supernormal profits being made in the short run and enter the industry, competing away these profits. Therefore, in the long run, monopolistically competitive firms will only make normal profits. At the profit-maximising level of output, $MC = MR$ and therefore the firm cannot be allocatively efficient ($P \neq MC$).

Question 10
Correct answer D

A monopolistically competitive firm will brand its products to ensure that they are slightly differentiated. Therefore, the hotel will seek to create brand loyalty to allow it to exercise some price-setting powers.

Option A would require a small number of firms to dominate (oligopoly). Option B suggests perfect competition. Option C suggests the firm is productively efficient and E suggests allocative efficiency, both of which are not possible under conditions of monopolistic competition.

Theory of the firm: oligopoly

Question 11
Correct answer A

In an oligopoly, firms produce similar products, which ensures that the firms are inter-dependent. If a firm raises the price of its chocolate, few suppliers will follow, so revenue will fall. Equally, if the manufacturer lowers prices, others will do so and a price war will result, ensuring that total revenue falls. Therefore, oligopolists will aim to avoid price changes and create brand loyalty through non-price competition, such as advertising or changes in packaging.

Question 12
Correct answer B

Concentration ratios can be defined as the market share controlled by the largest 'n' firms in the markets. In this case, the largest three firms control 46% of the market share.

A common mistake to make is to include 'others' among the leading firms. 'Others' refers to all other firms not included in the data, all of which have a market share smaller than the smallest named firm.

Question 13
Correct answer D

One of the characteristics of an oligopoly is that only a few firms dominate the market. Therefore, in an oligopoly, firms are more likely to collude and fix prices to avoid price wars.

Theory of the firm: monopoly

Question 14
Correct answer B (see Figures 7 and 18)
Profit maximisation occurs where a firm operates at $MC = MR$. Revenue maximisation occurs where $MR = 0$. Therefore, a firm moving from the objective of profit maximisation will increase output and, as a consequence, prices will fall.

Question 15
Correct answer B (see Figure 18)
A monopoly will always profit maximise on the elastic part of the average revenue or demand curve. We know this because the firm operates to the left of the revenue maximising point; that is, $MR = 0$, which is equivalent to an elasticity of 1, i.e. the mid-point on the average revenue curve.

Competition policy

Question 16
Correct answer C
The Competition Commission is governed by the Enterprise Act of 2002, which seeks to protect consumer interests through the promotion of competition. Sharp Corporation and LG Electronics were fined for price fixing because they behaved in an uncompetitive manner and therefore reduced consumer welfare. The fine was intended to prevent a repeat of this uncompetitive behaviour.

Question 17
Correct answer E
The Office of Fair Trading will request an investigation into a merger between two firms if they have a market share of 25% or more or if they meet the turnover test of a combined turnover of £70 million. The Competition Commission will block the merger if they feel that it would result in less competition and would, therefore, act against the best interests of the consumer.

Data-response questions

Question 1 Royal Mail must 'face the facts' of sell-off

Extract 1 *Royal Mail and potential sell-off*

Gordon Brown has told postal workers, unions and party rebels to 'face the facts' over Royal Mail's sell-off.

Deliveries of letters are falling fast as people use e-mail and other more modern forms of communication. But, as the number of purchases through the internet increases, package deliveries are on the rise. By 2013, Royal Mail expects that half of group revenues and three-quarters of its profits will come from its parcels division. However, during his keynote speech at the meeting, Brown was defiant and claimed the move was necessary for both the service's future and workers' pensions.

'I think we all recognise that the Royal Mail, which is part of the fabric of our country, faces huge challenges,' he said in a keynote speech to Labour's National Policy Forum.

'I ask you to consider the facts we have to face: there is an £8 billion deficit appearing in the pension fund of the Royal Mail; there is a loss of business of sometimes 7–8% each year as a result of new technology; there is a race to keep many of the very big customers who provide the majority of the work that the Royal Mail does.

I do say to you that guaranteeing a £25 billion pension fund, spending £1.9 billion on the Post Office network, maintaining a universal service obligation can be achieved if we make the investment that is necessary to secure the Royal Mail for the future.

And that is what is behind our proposals to get someone to help us invest so that we can prepare the Royal Mail for the international and national challenges ahead.'

Business secretary, Peter Mandelson, announced this week that around 30% of Royal Mail could be sold off to a foreign firm.

Sources: Adapted from 'Royal Mail must "face the facts" of sell-off' by Robin Henry, *The Times*, 28 February 2009 and 'Dutch frontrunner for Royal Mail accused of bullying workforce' by Tim Webb, *Guardian*, 10 March 2009

(a) **With reference to paragraph four, explain why the government wants to introduce foreign investment into the Royal Mail.** (4 marks)

(b) **Discuss two pricing and two non-pricing strategies that the Royal Mail could adopt to improve profitability.** (16 marks)

data-response question

(c) To what extent is mail delivery contestable? (10 marks)

(d) Evaluate whether further competition in the delivery service would
be in the best interests of consumers. (10 marks)

■ ■ ■

Candidate's answer

(a) First, there is an £8 billion hole in Royal Mail's pension fund that is increasing all the time. Foreign investment will help rectify this situation in two ways.

- First, it will provide the capital required to fill the hole.
- Second, it will bring expertise in managing large pension funds to the Royal Mail, which may help to prevent such a deficit occurring again.

The second reason why the government wants to introduce foreign investment to the Royal Mail is that it is losing 7–8% of its business each year. Foreign investment will help it to introduce the technologies into its infrastructure that are currently causing it to lose business. **4/4 marks**

> This type of answer requires the candidate only to refer to the extract to score full marks. Clearly, this candidate shows evidence of having read the text and making reference to it.

(b) First, Royal Mail could introduce greater price discrimination, particularly between businesses and private individuals. Price discrimination increases profit by charging those individuals whose demand is less elastic more for the same service. Given that business customers' demand for mail services tends to be fairly inelastic, charging them more money could increase profits. Profits could also be increased by charging people on the basis of when they receive their mail. People who want their mail early in the morning tend to be business customers, whose demand for mail services is inelastic. Therefore, charging these customers more would increase profits.

> The candidate may have considered drawing a price discrimination diagram like that in Figure 19. However, when drawing a diagram, consider whether it adds to the understanding of the examiner. Most of the time the answer is 'Yes', but in this case, unless you can draw Figure 19 in 30 seconds, it would be an enormous waste of time and, therefore, potential marks.

In evaluation, we should note that there would be significant costs in implementing such a system. First, large registers of Royal Mail customers would need to be set up to determine what qualified as business mail and what was not business mail. Furthermore, the number of postal rounds would have to be doubled; there would have to be one early postal round and one later one. This would increase costs, thereby limiting the increases in profit resulting from an increase in price discrimination.

Second, the Royal Mail could increase the amount it charges to send a letter. A great deal of mail has been made superfluous by the introduction of e-mail. There is, therefore, little competition in the market for letter distribution because it is a rapidly declining industry. This gives the Royal Mail significant price-making ability. Many of those who still send a lot of letters are people without computers. These people, therefore, have very inelastic demand for letter distribution. This means that the Royal Mail could use its price-making ability to raise prices to consumers with inelastic demand, thereby increasing profit.

In evaluation, it seems to be worth analysing who the customers are who send lots of letters. They are, by and large, businesses, government agencies and old people. Businesses and government agencies tend to attempt to lower their cost bases wherever possible, either to increase profits or because they are accountable to taxpayers. Therefore, if the Royal Mail starts charging more, they will simply start using other letter distributors. Old people tend to live on fixed incomes and therefore minimise unnecessary spending. If the cost of sending a letter goes up, they will probably send fewer letters. Therefore, the price elasticity of demand for letter distribution appears to be much more elastic than first suggested, making raising prices for stamps a bad strategy for increasing the Royal Mail's profitability.

> In the candidate's evaluation, the candidate could also have considered the split in customer bases — how many of the consumers of the Royal Mail are not business customers? Raising the price of stamps to the elderly may not be significant, even if demand from this group is relatively inelastic, as the group may represent a small proportion of the customer base.

One non-price strategy that the Royal Mail could introduce to improve its profitability would be to speed up the delivery of mail. Currently, the Royal Mail loses a lot of money to courier firms, because many people like to have next-day delivery of their mail guaranteed, which the Royal Mail cannot always do. By improving infrastructure, the Royal Mail could speed up delivery and therefore win customers back from courier agencies, thereby increasing profits.

In evaluation, this could increase the Royal Mail's cost base. In order to improve the speed of mail delivery, the Royal Mail would probably have to deploy more trains, vans and postmen. This would increase costs, thereby reducing the profitability of such an exercise.

Another non-price strategy that the Royal Mail could adopt to improve its profitability would be to reduce its cost base. Currently, the Royal Mail has a high cost base. If the Royal Mail were to reduce its workers' pay and fire excess labour, then it could reduce its labour costs and increase profits. **13/16 marks**

> This is an example of an excellent answer which has been well structured and developed. The candidate has considered two pricing and two non-pricing strategies, all of which score well for their focus on the Royal Mail. The candidate also evaluates each point as the points are covered and hence is able to ensure that

data-response question

any evaluation is always made in the context of the question and is therefore very relevant.

(c) A contestable market is one that is defined by low barriers to entry and exit and low sunk costs.

Ostensibly, the market for mail distribution appears to be fairly uncontestable. There are significant barriers to entry, in that the Royal Mail is effectively subsidised by the government, has massive brand power and benefits from significant economies of scale. Second, there are lots of barriers to exit, because workers cannot be fired without paying off their contracts.

In evaluation, we should point out that the barriers to entry are not as high as first supposed. First, the government's support for the Royal Mail is dwindling, as shown by the passage. Second, the Royal Mail's brand is often viewed with disdain by those who consider the company to be worn-out and inefficient. Finally, the Royal Mail also suffers from significant diseconomies of scale. In these respects, the market may actually be fairly contestable.

Sunk costs are those costs that cannot be retrieved upon exit from the market. There are very high sunk costs in the market for mail distribution because the industry is very labour intensive, and wages obviously cannot be recovered upon exit from the market. The machinery required for letter distribution is specific and is hard to sell on, given the fact that there are very few companies in the business. **7/10 marks**

This candidate has a good understanding of what is meant by contestability and starts the answer with a definition of the term to set the scene. The candidate does a good job of discussing the main issues that determine whether the mail delivery industry could be contestable, considering the types of sunk costs and attempting some evaluation. However, more evaluation could have been provided, especially when considering the significance of the level of sunk costs and their relative importance.

(d) On the one hand, competition should be in the interests of consumers. Competition should lead to lower prices for consumers, because firms have to compete to attract customers and will therefore lower price. Competition leads to a decrease in price-making ability and therefore to an increase in productive and allocative efficiency, as firms are forced to produce at the price set by the market.

However, this assumes that, with more competition, the market would move closer to the model of perfect competition. This is, of course, unrealistic. Given the complex, transnational nature of the letter distribution industry, it is unlikely that the market could support more than four or five firms. This would, in fact, make the market more like an oligopoly, giving the few firms that dominate the market the incentive to collude, to the detriment of the consumer.

On the other hand, competition could have detrimental effects. If a company has monopoly power, then it will be able to earn supernormal profits, which give it the means to increase research and development, and therefore to innovate. This can lead to new technologies emerging in mail distribution, which benefit the consumer. Second, if a company has monopoly power, it can benefit from economies of scale. The Royal Mail benefits from significant financial economies of scale. Because it has systemic importance for the economy and is backed by the government, the Royal Mail is a low credit risk and therefore benefits from relatively cheap loans. This lowers the prices that consumers pay.

In evaluation, we should note that the Royal Mail currently suffers from significant diseconomies of scale. It is so big and unwieldy that managers often have difficulty tracking mail going from one place to another. It has become so difficult logistically to control the Royal Mail that it is now productively inefficient. If other firms were to take market share from the Royal Mail as a result of competition, then it could become more efficient, benefiting consumers. **9/10 marks**

e The candidate understands the need to consider both the benefits of increased competition and why competition might not work. The candidate describes some of the benefits one might expect with competition but recognises that, in the case of the Royal Mail, this might not be beneficial, suggesting to an extent that the Royal Mail may be a natural monopoly. This leads on to a thoughtful discussion of why some industries are better off without competition, especially when competition leads to collusion among the dominant firms.

Total score: 33/40 = a good clear grade A

Question 2 Tesco wins appeal against Competition Commission test for new sites

Tesco's victory over competition ruling on expansion

Tesco yesterday won an appeal against a new competition test that would make it harder for the supermarket chain to open new stores or expand existing premises.

The Competition Appeal Tribunal (CAT) ruled that a competition test drawn up last April by the Competition Commission, the regulator, risked harming consumers because of unforeseen consequences. The commission had proposed the rule stipulating that permission for a new supermarket would be dependent upon a retailer's existing market share in the area — based on data provided by the Office of Fair Trading.

data-response question

Tesco asked for a judicial review of the proposal, arguing that the new test was unnecessary and that it would harm customers, rather than help them. It argued that the new test would simply add another hurdle to the planning approval process.

Tesco has a huge pipeline of properties that it hopes to turn into supermarkets and convenience stores to add to its 2,000-plus outlets. It says it will add 2 million sq ft (186 000 sq m) to its floor space by April 2010.

Overturning the decision, the CAT said that the Competition Commission had not fully assessed and taken into account the risk that the new test might harm consumers. It also said that the commission had not properly evaluated whether the costs of introducing the competition test would outweigh any benefits it might bring.

Source: Adapted from 'Tesco wins appeal against Competition Commission test for new sites' by Ian King,
The Times, 5 March 2009

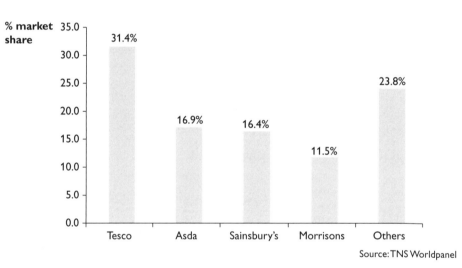

Source: TNS Worldpanel

Figure C UK supermarket share in 2008

(a) **With reference to the data, what market structure best describes the supermarket sector?** (4 marks)

(b) **To what extent can Tesco use its monopsony power to benefit the consumer?** (12 marks)

(c) **Evaluate the likelihood of collusion in the supermarket industry. Use game theory to support your answer.** (12 marks)

(d) **Discuss the role the Competition Commission plays in protecting the public interest.** (12 marks)

Candidate's answer

(a) The market has a four-firm concentration ration of 76.2%. The market is, therefore, best characterised as an oligopoly because it is dominated by a few large firms with significant price-making ability. **4/4 marks**

🖉 There is reference to and use of the data, and clear reference to oligopoly.

(b) Two points need to be analysed here. First, we need to examine how Tesco's monopsony power affects its cost base, and second we need to examine how changes in its cost base will translate into the price the consumer pays.

Monopsonies occur when a market has one large buyer and multiple sellers. This allows the buyer to drive down prices, as the sellers cannot sell to anyone, so they have to take the price offered by the buyer. This occurs with Tesco. Tesco has a degree of monopsony power; as the largest UK supermarket, Tesco can drive down the prices it pays for its products. Because farmers do not have many people to sell to, they will have to take the price Tesco offers them for their produce. This will cause the wholesale price of milk and other farm produce to fall, thereby lowering Tesco's cost base. This will allow Tesco to cut the prices that the consumer pays at the till.

However, if we continue our analysis, we will see that this is unlikely to happen. Tesco controls 31.4% of the UK food retail market. This affords Tesco's significant price-making ability. In many areas of the UK, the only supermarket accessible to people is a Tesco store, giving it local monopoly power. Because Tesco has little competition, it may decide to use the purchasing economies of scale that emerge from its monopsony power to increase profits, rather than cut prices for consumers. It does not need to pass on price cuts, because it has monopoly power.

In evaluation, we should question the extent of Tesco's monopsony power. After all, 68.6% of the UK food retail market is controlled by retailers who are not affiliated with Tesco. Furthermore, producers could export their produce to other supermarkets within the EU. Therefore, they don't necessarily have to take the price that Tesco offers them, thus limiting Tesco's monopsony power. **9/12 marks**

🖉 An accurate definition of monopsony is given with reference to the data presented. There is a clear explanation of how the firm may actually use this power to drive down prices charged to them by farmers. Excellent linkages are made here to Tesco's monopoly position, using Figure C to support this assertion, and therefore its price-setting power, as well as its position as a monopsony. This counts as evaluation, along with the reference to the extent to which Tesco has a monopsony. Top answers would have considered further the way in which Tesco could use its monopsony position to extract exclusivity deals and gain changes in delivery patterns and stock design.

(c) Collusion is best defined as tacit or explicit communication between competing companies that is to the detriment of the consumer.

data-response question

On the one hand, collusion in the supermarket sector would appear to be very likely. Because the market has a four-firm concentration ratio of 76.2%, the market is characterised by oligopoly and therefore firms can collude with great ease — there are only four, so organising price fixing would not be hard. Furthermore, the incentives to collude are strong. If firms collude to fix prices, then there is no competition and the market has the characteristics of a monopoly — the firms that constitute the oligopoly can agree to fix prices where $MC = MR$, thereby maximising profits. Therefore, they can all benefit from higher prices. This is reflected on the game theory matrix in the upper-left quadrant, where the parties both cooperate, leading to both parties succeeding. The total pay-off here is the largest the two firms could achieve working together. This is the highest possible pay-off, reflecting the collectively rational position. Therefore, firms benefit the most from colluding.

If the other firm cooperates, it is better to defect and cut your prices, thereby under-cutting the other firm, stealing its customers, increasing your profits and increasing your pay-off on the matrix. If the other firm defects by cutting prices in spite of the agreement, it is better to defect and cut your prices too, so your customers will not be stolen by the other firm. Therefore, even if collusion is mutually benefi-cial, it is always in the interests of the firms in the agreement to lower their prices and take business from the other firms, so collusion is unlikely to function in the long term.

In evaluation, it is worth noting the other principal reason for which collusion is unlikely in the supermarket sector: the Office of Fair Trading (OFT). The OFT is a government agency that is mandated to prevent firms from engaging in uncom-petitive practices that harm the consumer, such as price fixing and predatory pricing. If supermarkets all raise their prices in tandem without good justification, such as an increase in wholesale food prices, then the OFT can look into the price increases, and fine them if it finds them to have engaged in price fixing. These fines can be very large and therefore act as a strong disincentive to collude.

12/12 marks

✐ The candidate makes good use of the 2 × 2 matrix referred to in the Content Guidance section of this book under 'Oligopoly'. The candidate clearly understands the implications of the 2 × 2 matrix, which suggests that there are clear incentives to be had from breaking any collusive agreement and trying to maximise your own individual benefits, especially before the authorities have been alerted to such behaviour.

(d) The Competition Commission is a government office that oversees mergers and acquisitions within the UK and prevents integration where it feels that it will be to the detriment of the consumer's interests.

The Competition Commission automatically oversees any merger that will give the resulting firm a share of the market that exceeds 25%. It may approve of mergers that give firms a large share of the market if they feel that this will lead to benefits to the consumer. Indeed, the commission does seem to feel that mergers that create groups with large market share can be beneficial. The commission allowed the acquisition of Colour Care Ltd by Kodak, on the grounds that the new firm would be more capable of fostering technological innovation, which would benefit the consumer.

The commission does, however, remain wary of the dangers of certain mergers. When BSkyB tried to merge with Manchester United Football Club in 1998, the commission prohibited the merger, on the grounds that it might lead to BSkyB charging high prices to watch pay-per-view footage of Manchester United games. This would have harmed the consumer; prices would have risen with no other benefits emerging, so the commission prevented it.

In evaluation, we should note that the Competition Commission has been willing to play down the importance of competition in a difficult economic climate. The commission approved the merger of Lloyds TSB with HBOS in 2008, despite the fact that the merger gave the new group significant price-making ability, because it felt that it was more important to safeguard the interests of depositors at HBOS. **8/12 marks**

The candidate makes reference to a number of examples from past Edexcel questions (Unit number 6354, paper 01) to support their answer and explain how the Competition Commission would seek to protect consumers. The candidate also refers to contemporary data in the form the Lloyds TSB/HBOS merger in 2008 to show that the Competition Commission had to compromise its pro-competition remit in the economic climate of late 2008 and early 2009. Top candidates could well have discussed the meaning of public interest and related it to the need for competition as determined by the Enterprise Act.

Total score: 33/40 = a good clear grade A

Question 3 Trains cost 50% more than in rest of Europe

Cost of rail fares in Britain

Rail fares in Britain are on average 50% higher than the rest of Europe, a study has shown, putting pressure on rail operators and the government to cut ticket prices.

Annual season tickets for middle-distance commuters are almost double the price of the next most expensive country, France, and more than four times that of the cheapest country, Italy.

Ruth Kelly commissioned Passenger Focus, the consumer watchdog, to carry out the inquiry last year when she was transport secretary. She had noticed that customer satisfaction levels had not risen in line with improvements in train performance.

data-response question

> Anthony Smith, chief executive of Passenger Focus, said the study confirmed that British fares were 'astonishingly expensive, especially for tickets that you buy on the day and especially for commuters in London and the south-east'.
>
> However, it was not all bad news for British travellers. Passengers willing to make advance purchases can buy some of the cheapest tickets available in Europe and British trains run more frequently, with passenger services starting earlier and finishing later than their Continental rivals. The findings brought new calls for the government to revise plans to cut rail subsidies. The government aims to get passengers to foot three-quarters of the cost of operating and improving the network — a rise from £5 billion per year now to £9 billion by 2014.
>
> 'The government should review its intention to shift the cost of funding the railway from taxpayers to passengers,' said Mr Smith, 'Passengers cannot be expected to continue paying above-inflation fare increases year on year during the recession.'

Source: from 'Trains cost 50% more than in rest of Europe' by Gill Plimmer, *Financial Times*, 19 February 2009

(a) To what extent are the railways in the UK an example of a natural monopoly? (8 marks)

(b) Discuss whether wider use of price regulation may benefit railway passengers. (12 marks)

(c) Evaluate the impact of a reduction in the state-provided subsidy for the railway companies. (10 marks)

(d) Assess why rail prices in the UK might be significantly higher than those in Europe. (10 marks)

■ ■ ■

Candidate's answer

(a) A natural monopoly is a monopoly that occurs naturally in an economy because the market cannot support more than one firm. The railways are an example of a natural monopoly because there is only one railway company — Network Rail — which supplies the tracks. There are really high costs to setting up a rival firm and no one would try to establish another rail line because it will costs lots and take a long time before any expenditure is recovered. **4/8 marks**

> ⓔ This candidate has some understanding of what is meant by a natural monopoly but lacks the technical expertise that one would expect to see from an A-grade candidate, such as reference to high barriers to entry and high sunk costs. The answer would have benefited from a diagram (see Figure 20), which could have been used to explain and support the answer. The use of 'To what extent' in the

question suggests that some evaluation is necessary and the candidate has not done this. The best option for some evaluation would be to compare the role of Network Rail, which is clearly a natural monopoly, with the train-operating companies, where there is clearly some scope for competition.

(b) Prices can be regulated using the RPI – X formula in order to ensure that prices may increase in nominal terms, but they will tend to fall in real terms. The regulator will set prices in such a way as to ensure that the train operator will be able to make a profit, but will have to make efficiency savings and improvements in quality if they are to increase their profits. This will happen because the train operator can keep any profits they make after they have cut costs.

The benefits of this system are that it allows the rail operator to keep any profits that it makes, but ensures that there is an incentive to improve the quality of service and to get more passengers on board the trains. However, it is quite possible that a cut in costs will equate to a cut in customer service, as the drive to make efficiency gains and increase profits to satisfy the demands of shareholders outweighs the desire to maintain quality of service, particularly as demand for trains is often seen to be relatively price inelastic. **7/12 marks**

The candidate has an understanding of the demands of the regulator and how the regulator may actually meet these. There is an explanation of how this may work and how prices will actually fall. However, there is limited explanation of how this regulation may actually help consumers. Furthermore, with very low inflation at the time the article was written, the possibility of nominal as well as real price cuts is real. This may mean that the regulator's actions, while resulting in price cuts, may actually lead to deterioration in the quality of service.

The candidate discusses quality of service but could also have mentioned regulatory capture as one possible downside of regulation; they could have tried to compare the UK method of regulation with other types of regulation (these are now included in the specification); or mentioned the need for rail operators to spend on capital and therefore referred to the possibility of using RPI + K.

(c) The subsidy received from the state helps to ensure that prices remain low and therefore encourage consumers to use the railways. A reduction in the state subsidy is, therefore, likely to put pressure on the train operators either to cut costs or raise prices. As they have probably been forced to cut costs by the regulator over the years, it is clear that the only feasible alternative is to raise prices. This will put pressure on already hard-pressed consumers. They are likely to consider alternatives to the train, although road transport is also becoming more expensive and therefore less attractive. The state has been keen to reduce the size of the subsidy for some time, encouraging the private sector to take greater responsibility for the cost of running the railways, but this will no doubt put some routes that the private sector runs under even greater pressure. It is much harder for the state to force firms to run loss-making routes and cross-subsidise these with the profits from other routes if the state makes no contribution. Undoubtedly at some

data-response question

point, consumers will feel resentful over the fact that service has declined and they have to pay more so that they can provide a service that they are unlikely ever to need. **7/10 marks**

This is a good answer, which addresses the main issues surrounding a reduction in the subsidy and the possible outcomes in the form of resentment, loss of certain routes, poorer customer service and higher prices. The candidate could also have considered whether the subsidy was actually needed any more and whether the firms were now in a position to stand on their own feet. Furthermore, the subsidy could have acted as a disincentive to improve efficiency and it is only with this reduction that the firms can improve. Although prices have been rising and are the highest in Europe, this has not yet had an effect on demand and it may be possible to raise prices further without consumer demand declining significantly.

(d) Rail prices in Britain are the highest in Europe. The article states that prices in the UK are almost double those of France, the next most expensive supplier, and almost four times the price of the Italian railways. This may be the case for a number of reasons.

It may be the case that the subsidy in the UK is significantly less than that of the other members of the European Union and therefore rail passengers must pay a larger proportion of the cost of operating the railways.

On the other hand it may be the case that the railways in Britain have invested larger amounts to ensure a better quality of train and service. This may be the reason why British trains run more frequently and are more punctual.

Furthermore, consumers may be willing to pay more for the railways because there are few reliable and price-competitive substitutes. The car may be a more expensive alternative and the establishment of the congestion charge and increased traffic means that the demand for the railways is relatively price inelastic.

6/10 marks

The candidate has managed to identify three reasons why the prices may be higher in Britain compared to the rest of Europe, but does very little evaluation. Evaluation may have included some reference to profiteering or a benign regulator allowing the train operators to raise prices. It may also be the case that the train operating companies are colluding to fix prices and therefore maximise their own profits. Government subsidies clearly play a role, but are these the most significant factor? Perhaps British rail operators run more cost-ineffective services (the article states that they are more frequent) than their European rivals and so need to recoup the cost through higher prices.

Total 24/40 = most likely a grade C. The lack of evaluation here damages the candidate's mark. Evaluation is crucial in ensuring that a candidate accesses the full range of marks and achieves a top grade.